The World's Best Business Jokes

The World's Best Business Jokes

Charles Alverson

Illustrated by Tony Blundell

ANGUS
& ROBERTSON
PUBLISHERS

(ZZ9DEC5660)

Imprint page – The World's Best Business Jokes – B37 – 5660

ANGUS & ROBERTSON PUBLISHERS

*16 Golden Square, London W1R 4BN,
United Kingdom, and
Unit 4, Eden Park, 31 Waterloo Road,
North Ryde, NSW, Australia 2113*

*First published in the United Kingdom by
Angus & Robertson (UK) in 1989
First published in Australia by
Angus & Robertson Publishers in 1989
Reprinted 1990*

*Text copyright © Charles Alverson, 1989
Illustrations copyright © Tony Blundell, 1989*

*British Library Cataloguing in Publication Data
Alverson, Charles
    The world's best business jokes
    I. Title
    828'.91402*

ISBN 0 207 16385 5

*Typeset in Great Britain by New Faces, Bedford
Printed in Great Britain by BPCC Hazell Books Ltd, Aylesbury*

To my daughter Clare, without whose help and research
this could have been a very short collection
of business jokes indeed.

'I still don't know what makes my boss tick,' said the secretary in the cafeteria, 'but I've learned what makes him explode.'

The proprietor of the factory was so mean with the heating that one day he found a note pinned to the fire alarm: 'In case of fire, keep it to yourself or everyone will want one.'

Tax inspector to nervous businessman: 'Now, tell me again how you thought it was legal to claim depreciation on your mother-in-law.'

'I'm very sorry, sir,' the bookkeeper told his employer, 'that you can't manage to give me a rise. Several companies are after me, you know.'
    'And what companies might those be?' asked his boss.
    'The electric company, the gas company, the telephone company ...'

While interviewing a potential client, the executive switched on his intercom and commanded: 'Miss Willis! Get my broker on the telephone.'

'Yes, sir,' responded his secretary, 'stock or pawn?'

Boss to most junior employee: 'Tell me, Hobart, what is the main purpose of a holiday?'

Hobart: 'To impress upon the employee that the company can get along without him.'

Needing a bit of cash, Tarzan decided to go into the used crocodile business. The next morning, he got up early, went down to the river bank and spent a long day haggling over dodgy crocks.

When he swung back to the tree hut that evening, he demanded: 'Quick, Jane, make me a martini!' He downed it in a gulp and urged: 'Another one.' That martini followed the first, and Tarzan held out his glass and gasped: 'One more!'

'But, Tarzan,' said Jane worriedly, 'you mustn't overdo it.'

'You don't understand, Jane,' said Tarzan urgently. 'It's a *jungle* out there.'

The boss had to make a speech at an important convention and asked Jenkins, his personal assistant, to write him a punchy twenty-minute speech. The PA did so, but when his boss returned to the office he was very angry and called for Jenkins.

'You fool,' he said, 'I asked for a twenty-minute speech, and you not only gave me one that was an hour long but was so boring that half the audience was asleep before I was finished. How could you do this to me?'

At first Jenkins was baffled, but then he replied: 'I did write the speech you requested,' he said, 'but, if you'll recall, I also gave you two carbon copies of it.'

Secretary: 'What's your new boss like?'
Other secretary: 'Not my typing, that's for sure.'

At the office Christmas party, the boss was demo-cratically playing bartender, and the wife of one of the company executives seemed to be making an awful lot of trips to the bar. Finally, her husband warned her: 'That's the tenth drink you've had in the last hour. What will my boss think of you?'

'That's okay,' she reassured him. 'Every time I order a drink, I tell him it's for you.'

Al, a small businessman, suddenly found himself inundated with huge bills that he simply couldn't pay, so he went to his brother-in-law, Bert, and asked for a loan to save his business.

'Sorry,' said his brother-in-law, 'you're a bad risk.'

'But, Bert,' Al said, 'when you were broke I gave you a job.'

'That's right.'

'I introduced you to my sister and talked her into marrying you.'

'That's true,' Bert said.

'And when you said you were tired of being an employee, I set you up in business and even recommended you to my customers.'

'I know, Al, I know,' Bert said, 'but what have you done for me lately?'

The company chairman, about to attempt a putt on the twelfth hole, noticed a funeral procession passing and suddenly paused. He placed his cap over his heart and waited until the procession was out of sight before taking a sight on the ball again.

'That's very touching, J.B.,' said his playing partner. 'You're a sentimental devil.'

'It was the least I could do,' J.B. said, holing the

putt. 'Next Saturday would have been our thirtieth wedding anniversary.'

The new employee had been with the firm for only a couple of weeks when she went in to see her boss and asked for a raise.

'What?' demanded the boss, 'So soon? Of course not. To get more money with this firm, you must work yourself up.'

'I have! I have!' insisted the employee. 'Look at me; I'm trembling all over.'

The company offered its employees a course for prospective executives describing it as follows: 'This course is for people who have a hard time making decisions day in and day out. This is not a stuffy, stifling approach to problem-solving. So don't register if you think you have all the answers. If you don't know whether you want to sign up for this course, you are eligible.'

The brand-new apprentice was excited on his first day with the local garage and was amazed when his boss told him: 'Put away those tools. The first thing you have to learn is how to open the car's bonnet and shake your head sadly.'

The pretty young college graduate was hired as personal assistant to a middle-aged business executive. She found that she had to travel a lot with him on business and was dismayed when he insisted on acting as if she was his girlfriend. Whenever they ate in a restaurant, he would call her 'darling' or 'dear' in front of the waiters.

At first she was patient, hoping that he would grow tired of it. But then, as they were entering an especially high-class restaurant she decided to take action. As the headwaiter approached to seat them, the boss asked her: 'Where do you want to sit, sweetheart?'

'Anywhere you like, Daddy,' the girl replied.

'Nobody likes hard work better than the person who pays for it.'

The boss of a small factory was notorious for his pose of aloofness in front of his employees.

But one day, his wife dropped by his office unexpectedly and greeted him with a kiss and a loving embrace.

Said one girl from the typing pool to another as their employer hurriedly shut his office door: 'The boss better be careful. We might start thinking he's human.'

The inspector from the Inland Revenue had a tip for the corporate treasurers he has to visit: 'The trick is to stop thinking of it as *your* money.'

Gerald and Cecil were dealers with rival City firms, so the first person Gerald called on the new cellular phone in his sports car was Cecil.

Seriously jealous, Cecil had a telephone installed in *his* sports car and immediately rang the number in Gerald's car. 'Gerald,' he exclaimed breezily, 'I'm calling you from my brand-new cellular car phone, and mine has a sixty-number memory and two speakers.'

'That's wonderful, Cecil,' Gerald said, 'but can you hang on for a moment? My other phone is ringing.'

The business executive was explaining why he'd hired one junior executive rather than another who, on the surface, seemed much better qualified.

'Well,' he said, 'when I interviewed Perkins, I was soon convinced that he was just about the smartest person in the world.'

'That sounds great,' said his colleague. 'So why did you hire Johnson?'

'Well,' said the executive, 'when I was interviewing Johnson, I was soon convinced that *I* was just about the smartest person in the world.'

Personnel director to job applicant: 'Not only do we have an excellent retirement plan, but if you come to work here you'll age a lot faster.'

The secretary of a tennis-mad lawyer could never think of a truthful way to answer calls when her boss was absent from the office. But now she just tells people: 'He's in court.'

A rich businessman was having dinner in a restaurant when he suddenly started choking on a fishbone. Fortunately, a surgeon was at a nearby table, and he quickly moved in and saved the businessman from death by asphyxiation. When he could talk again, the fortunate victim asked the surgeon how much he expected as a fee.

Replied the surgeon: 'Just give me one-third of what you were willing to pay when that fish-bone was still stuck in your throat.'

The head of a stationery firm despaired of ever getting his account paid by one of his biggest customers. Finally, he enclosed with a final reminder a picture of his three children and a note: 'This is the reason why I need the money so urgently.'

A response came back quickly with a photograph of a sexy blonde in a bikini under which was written: 'And this is the reason why I can't pay.'

One afternoon, the executive's wife came out into their front hallway to find her husband standing next to the hat rack with his hat in his hand and a puzzled expression on his face.

'Why, what's the matter, dear?' she enquired.

'I couldn't remember,' he said, 'whether I was going to work late or getting home early.'

'Why did you leave your last position?' the personnel director of the dress shop asked the prospective employee.

'Well,' said the applicant honestly, 'after a customer tried on absolutely every dress in the shop and didn't like any of them, she asked me if I didn't think she'd look better in something flowing. I agreed.'

'That doesn't sound so awful.'

'No,' said the job applicant, 'but unfortunately I suggested the river.'

Printed on a cardboard sign next to the pitch of a sidewalk tie salesman: 'Twenty minutes at this location.'

One worried businessman to another over their fifth martini: 'We know they're buying our shares, but the only problem is that we can't decide whether it's the thin end of the wedge or the tip of the iceberg.'

The estate agent was determined to sell the young couple a house he'd had on his list for an awful long time. They seemed to like it, but just as they were leaving the house, something flew over the fence and shattered a front window.

'What on earth was that?' demanded the husband.

'That's another advantage,' said the estate agent, thinking fast. 'You're only a stone's throw from the local school.'

Have you heard about the butcher who backed into the bacon-slicing room and got a little behind in his customer's orders?

The grocer advertised for a boy to work 'partly indoors and partly outdoors', and a very suitable boy applied and was hired. But the boy looked rather worried:

'Is something bothering you?' asked the grocer.

'Yes, sir,' the boy replied: 'What happens to me if somebody shuts the door?'

An elderly shopkeeper was dying, and his loving family gathered around his bedside.

Suddenly, the old man roused and asked: 'Is Joseph here?'

'Yes, father, I'm here,' said Joseph.

'Is Amy here?' the dying grocer demanded.

'Yes, dear,' said his wife. 'I'm right here.'

'Is Barbara here?' the old man persisted.

'Yes, grandfather,' the young girl said. 'We're here. We're all here.'

Suddenly the grocer sat bolt upright in bed and shouted: 'Then, who the hell is looking after the shop?'

The recently deceased arrived in heaven and on being asked his name replied: 'Sid. Sid Bodger.'

The angel on the gate, looked into his ledger and said: 'I can't find any appointment for you. What was your business on earth.'

'Scrap metal merchant,' Sid said.

'I'll go and enquire,' said the angel, but when he returned, Sid was gone. And so were the Pearly Gates.

Did you hear about the secretary who was so dumb that she wore a very long bead necklace so that her boss would know that he could count on her?

A shopkeeper was dismayed when a brand new business, much like his own, opened in the premises on the left side of his and erected a huge sign: BEST VALUES. He felt even worse when another similar business moved into the shop on the right side of his own and erected an even bigger sign: LOWEST PRICES. The shopkeeper was afraid that he was going to be driven out of business until he got a bright idea: He simply put an even bigger sign over his own front door reading: MAIN ENTRANCE.

'You think *your* business is bad?' said the depressed shopkeeper to a crony. 'Even my customers who never pay have stopped ordering.'

The woman liked the look of the chicken she was offered in the poultry shop, but it seemed a bit on the small side for all the company she had coming to dinner. 'Haven't you one a little larger?' she asked.
  'Just a second,' said the merchant, going into the

back room. But since he didn't have any more chickens that day he just plumped the bird up, pulled it this way and that until it looked a little bigger. Returning to his customer he showed her the chicken and said: 'How's that?'

'Fine,' said the woman, 'but on second thoughts, I'll take both of them.'

A customer from out of town went into a shop in a sleepy small town and found not a single customer but just the proprietor and a single salesman tipped back on a stool reading a newspaper.

As he paid for his small purchase, the stranger said: 'I hope you won't mind, but I can't help wondering how you manage to keep this place going if you don't have more business than this.'

'Well,' drawled the man behind the cash register, 'you see that fellow over there? He works for me, but I can't pay him. So, in two years he'll get ownership of the store. Then I'll work for him until I get it back again.'

The Complaints Manager of a department store arrived at his office to find an irate letter from a customer complaining that he'd bought an expensive barometer in the store but that when he'd got it home he found that the barometer's needle was stuck permanently on HURRICANE.

The executive put the letter on his 'Things to Handle Pretty Directly' tray, but before he could do anything about it the second post brought yet another letter from the barometer-buying customer.

'Dear Sir,' it said, 'please ignore my letter of complaint about the barometer I bought from you. When I got home from mailing it at the pillar box, not only was the barometer gone, but so was my entire house.'

The insurance agent was surprised one day when a famous but not very highly regarded singer came into the office and demanded to take out a policy on his voice.

'For how much?' asked the agent.

'A million pounds,' said the singer proudly.

'Well, sir,' said the agent, 'this is very unusual, but perhaps if you sang something for me, it would help us to decide.'

The singer obliged with one of his most popular numbers and then said: 'Well? What do you think?'

After a slight pause, the insurance agent told the singer: 'I'm afraid we can't help you. You really should have come to us before you had the accident.'

Searching for an accountant, the shopkeeper looked in the telephone book and saw the name of the firm – Jones, Jones, Jones & Jones. Dialling, he asked: 'Is Mr Jones there?'

'No,' said a man's voice, 'he's on holiday.'

'All right, then,' said the shopkeeper, 'let me speak to Mr Jones.'

'Sorry, he's out on a business call.'

'What about Mr Jones?' the man insisted.

'He's at lunch.'

'Well,' said the shopkeeper, getting impatient, 'give me Mr Jones.'

'Speaking.'

An executive ran into a former colleague who'd left the firm to become self-employed. 'How's it going?' he asked.

'To tell the truth,' said his friend, 'I never knew how stupid bosses could be until I started working for myself.'

Sign in an optician's shop: 'Trust us – we get spectacular results.'

Two businessmen went on safari to Africa, and the first thing they were warned about was going alone into the jungle. But after a week, they got over-confident and plunged into the bush by themselves.

They'd got no more than a few yards when a ferocious growl froze them in their tracks.

'Tom,' said one worried businessman, 'did you hear that?'

'I heard it, Jack,' said the other with a quaver in his voice.

The menacing sound came closer and closer.

'Jack,' trembled Tom, 'I can feel its hot breath. Take a look behind me – please!'

'I am – I am,' said Jack, his eyes growing large.

'Well?' demanded his friend, 'what is it? Is it a lion? Is it a tiger?'

'How should I know?' moaned Jack. 'I'm an iron-monger, not a furrier.'

The advertising agency was looking for a new account handler and advertised in the trade papers. They got three very promising replies, and the top brass gathered to select one of them to get the job.

After considerable argument, the agency president pronounced: 'Well, I say we choose this chap Smithers. He's not afraid to show impatience that he's not being appreciated where he is.' He picked up the applicant's letter and read: 'After eight years with this agency I am not in a senior position.'

'Now here,' said the boss, 'is a man bursting to show what he can do. Hire him.'

The agency did, and the new man lived up to their hopes, but then one day over lunch the president revealed exactly why they'd chosen him.

'You're not going to believe this,' said the new man, 'but you hired me because of a typing error. What I'd meant to say was: "After eight years with this agency, I am *now* in a senior position."'

Househunter: 'All of the properties you've shown us are too expensive. Don't you have anything in the price range I first suggested?'

Estate Agent: 'Well, yes, there is one, and I'd sell it to you, but we'd have to make a wirehaired terrier homeless.'

The lowly employee mustered his courage and marched into his immediate superior's office: 'I want a pay rise,' he said.

'Well, Tompkins,' said the boss, 'due to the fluctuational predisposition of your historical productive capacity as juxtaposed against your personal compensatory pattern, in my judgement it would be fiscally injudicious to enhance your increment.'

'Huh?' demanded the stunned underling. 'I don't get it.'

'Exactly,' said his boss.

After telling the customer all about the marvellous gadgets on a brand-new car, the salesman asked: 'Is there anything else I can explain for you?'

'Yes,' said the puzzled customer. 'Why is the £11,000 price you're asking for the car *modest* when the £200 discount you're offering me is *substantial?*'

When the House of Rothschild was engineering the merger of Charrington the brewers with their rival, Hoare & Co., the autocratic Lord Rothschild looked in on the negotiations. Seeing a long list of properties owned by the company being taken over, he enquired of a Rothschild banker: 'Are these Hoare houses?'

'No, my lord,' answered the minion with a diplomatically straight face, 'They're public houses.'

After days of head-to-head negotiations with the management, the shop stewards emerged from the conference room looking very pleased with themselves. Confidently, the senior shop steward addressed a mass meeting of workers.

'From now on,' he proclaimed, 'you'll get double wages, two months' holiday, two-hour lunch breaks and, what's even better, you only have to work one day a week – Friday.'

'What?' came a voice from the back, '*every* Friday?'

Plaque on the wall of a City boardroom: 'Thank heavens this is a free country where one can do exactly as the Government pleases.'

The giant company prided itself on keeping in touch with all of its thousands of employees however remote, even its sales rep on the most isolated of the Scottish Isles. One winter day in the middle of a snow-

storm, the rep watched through binoculars as the island postman fought through towering waves in his tiny boat and then hiked through deep drifts up the high hill to the rep's house. As he opened the door, the half-frozen postman handed him a letter.

As the postman was attempting to thaw out, the rep opened the letter which read: 'There is no corporate communication for you this week.'

The horsedealer couldn't believe his luck when he heard that Prince Valiant, a big winner at the tracks that season, was for sale. 'I'm pleased, of course,' he told the horse's owner, 'but how can you sell such a successful horse?'

'Ah,' said Prince Valiant's owner, 'I'm fed up with him. He's such a ham. Last week he was winning by a mile when he slowed down at the finishing line just to get in on a photo finish. And even then he turned his head to give the camera his best profile.'

'I don't care if he think he's Lord Olivier,' said the dealer. 'I'll take him.'

So the seller lead the buyer to the stable and called: 'Prince, this is your new owner. Get up and show him your impression of a lame horse.'

The fisherman brought a huge armful of angling paraphernalia up to the cash register, and watched with dismay as the shop assistant rang up over a hundred pounds' worth of gear. Sighing heavily, the fisherman was about to sign his cheque when he looked up and said: 'You know, if you started selling fish here, you could save me an awful lot of money.'

Famous business fibs:

We service what we sell.
Let's have lunch some time.
We've got your application on file.
It's nothing personal, just business.
One size fits all.

While the boss was out at a long lunch, half a dozen of his senior executives met at the vice president's office to figure out some way to ease the old man out of the driver's seat.

But suddenly the vice president's secretary came in and said: 'The chairman's here to see you.'

'My God,' said an executive, 'if he catches us here, he'll know we're up to something. Quick! Five of us will have to jump out of the window.'

'But we're on the thirteenth floor,' protested the company treasurer.

'Jump!' insisted the executive. 'This is no time for superstition.'

On first blush, the applicant for a job didn't impress the company's personnel manager. He explained that he'd been a circus juggler for ten years. In fact, he'd never done anything but juggle.

'But,' asked the personnel manager, 'if you're a juggler, why do you want to switch to a nine-to-five job?'

The applicant began a long-winded justification of this career change but then admitted: 'I'm fed up with bumming around with circuses, and I'm trying desperately to get into a rut.'

Question: Does a good reference from your boss mean he thinks a lot of you or that he just wants to get rid of you?'

Business Tip:
For a quick energy boost, nothing beats having the boss walk into your office.

The businessman was ordered to attend a conference for his company on such short notice that he didn't have time to write his speech, much less rehearse it. Once he'd arrived at his hotel, he settled down to write it and found that it was after midnight before he'd finished. Blinking back the urge to sleep, he began rehearsing the speech – over and over.

Finally, just after 2 a.m., he wearily began again the opening words of his speech. But no sooner had be begun than someone in the next room cleared his throat emphatically and said in a loud and determined tone: 'And finally ...!'

The housewife greeted the door-to-door watch salesman by saying: 'You're wasting your time. I don't need a watch.'

The salesman put down his two huge suitcases and said: 'But madam, you haven't seen what this little watch can do.' He pushed a button, and the watch said clearly: 'The time is 11:15 in the morning.'

'That's pretty impressive,' said the woman, 'but I don't want a watch.'

He pushed another button and the dial became a tiny television screen.

'I'm sorry,' the woman began, but the salesman pushed another button, and the watch produced beautiful, clear, loud stereo music.

'All right, all right, said the woman, 'I'll take it,' and she wrote out a hefty cheque which the man pocketed and walked away leaving his large suitcases on the doorstep.

'Wait!' cried the woman, 'you forget your sample cases.'

'Those aren't sample cases,' called the salesman. 'They're the batteries for the watch.'

Company first aid instructor: 'What telephone number would you dial if your employer had a heart attack?'

Disgruntled secretary: '998'.

Executive Plaque: 'I know you believe you understood what you think I said, but I'm not sure you realise what you heard is not what I meant to say.'

Mechanic to worried motorist: 'What'll it be: my guess for £10 or a computerised diagnosis for £50?'

The snow outside was getting deeper and deeper, and the salesman peered worriedly into the whiteness. 'Do you think,' he asked a stranger, 'that the roads are clear enough to get out and make some sales?'

'That depends,' said the stranger, 'on whether you're working on salary or on commission.'

Business Plaque: 'It's no longer the principle that counts; it's the interest.'

On the morning after the Stock Market took a big plunge, a client called his stockbroker: 'How do you feel today? Bullish or bearish?

'Neither,' said the financial wizard, 'sheepish'.

The English salesman's appointment with a very important customer in Edinburgh was so early that he had no choice but to take the overnight train. The only problem was that he always had a terrible time getting up in the morning, so he summoned the sleeping car porter and gave him £5.

'Now, listen,' he told the porter, 'I have to get off the train at 8 a.m. in Edinburgh. No matter what I say,

or do, just get me up, get me dressed and throw me off
the train, and I'll be eternally grateful.'

'I understand, sir,' said the porter, pocketing the
fiver, and the salesman got into his upper berth with an
easy mind. The next thing he knew, it was bright
daylight outside and he looked out of his berth to see
the station sign: Aberdeen. He'd overslept and now had
no chance of making that all important appointment.

Livid with anger, he found the porter, grabbed him
by the throat and raged: 'You promised! You promised
you'd get me off the train in Edinburgh, but you didn't,
and now you've ruined my career. I'll kill you!'

'I – I can understand your anger, sir,' stuttered the
porter, 'but just imagine how that fellow feels who I
threw off the train in Edinburgh.'

The lawyer brought a very long and complex contract
he'd written to his boss. After the boss had been
reading some time, he looked up and said: 'It's a shame
your work doesn't get read more often, Barclay. Your
small print is superb.'

The magazine's article about a suburban town included the memorable line: 'The town centre has an impressive selection of shops, banks and other places of worship.'

Desk Sign: 'You may not think much of what I say, but remember that it is one four-thousand millionth of the world's opinion.'

A burglar was discovered rifling the safe in an Inland Revenue office and was subdued after a considerable struggle by a tax inspector. The police collected the burglar, the inspector was congratulated and that was considered the end of the matter until a detective rang from the local police station.

'It's about that burglar you caught,' he told the tax inspector. We found £50 in his pockets.'

'Yes?' said the tax inspector. 'What about it?'

'Well,' said the detective, 'he swears that when he broke into your office he had £65 on him.'

At the office coffee dispenser, a colleague warned Jenkins: 'That's your third cup this morning. Haven't you been reading what doctors have been saying about the dangers of drinking coffee?'

'Yes,' said Jenkins, 'and I'm quite worried about it, but I don't see what that has to do with the stuff that comes out of this machine.'

The factory manager began to realise just how bad unemployment was in his area when he advertised for workers. Three quarters of the applicants filled in the 'Salary Expected' blank with the word: 'Yes.'

The boss was a keen yachtsman, and everyone in the office had chipped in to buy him a sextant as a birthday present. Smith volunteered to buy it. Since the ships chandler had run out of them, Smith rang the local sporting goods shop. After a short conversation, he hung up the phone with a bemused expression on his face.

'What's the matter?' someone asked him.

'Well,' said Smith, 'I asked the girl who answered whether she had a sextant in stock and she told me that they had all kinds of tents, and if I bought one what I did in it was entirely my own business.'

The man in the queue at the bank suddenly developed a terrible case of hiccups just as his turn came to be served.

'I wonder – hic –' he said, 'if – hic – you could – hic – hic – tell me the – hic – balance of my – hic – hic – bank account.'

The teller went away from the window for a moment and then returned, saying: 'I'm sorry, but your account is overdrawn by £10,000.'

'What!' cried the customer. 'You must be joking.'

'Yes, I am,' admitted the teller, 'but your hiccups are gone now, aren't they?'

The company chairman was a hard-headed character who seldom admitted a doubt about the value of his opinions.

Finally, one day a braver-than-most executive bearded him: 'You always think you're right, but there must have been times when you've been wrong. Admit it?'

'Well, yes,' confessed the chairman. 'I was wrong once.'

'When was that?'

'Well,' said the boss, 'some years back I made an important decision which I thought was wrong, but in the end it wasn't.'

The Post Office employee was retiring after thirty years, and his supervisor called him into the office. 'Joe,' he said, 'you've been here longer than any of us and experienced a lot. What would you say you've learned in thirty years with us?'

Joe thought for a moment and said: 'Don't post my gold watch. I'll take it with me.'

An executive and his wife were entertaining his boss to dinner at a restaurant when the executive began to tell a joke which she thought might be a bit too risqué for the boss, a very religious man. She gave her husband a kick under the table, but he continued telling the joke. She gave him an even harder kick, but he ploughed on regardless. The wife was about to kick him yet again when suddenly the husband stopped telling the joke and changed the subject.

While the boss was away from the table, she whispered: 'Why didn't you stop telling that awful joke the first time I kicked you?'

'But, I did,' the husband protested. 'I did'.

Suddenly, the wife realised that it *hadn't* been her husband she'd been kicking, but when their guest came back to the table, he put them at their ease: 'Don't worry. After the second kick, I realised that it wasn't for me, so I passed it on.'

'I don't really know whether this fellow is being sarcastic or not,' said the bank manager showing his assistant an application from a customer: 'If you can see your way clear to giving me an overdraft, I will be forever in your debt.'

The boss dictated an important notice to his secretary.

'Shall I put this on the notice board?' she asked.

'Of course not,' said the boss. 'Put it on the office clock. I want everybody to see it.'

The owner of a dry-cleaning shop wondered why everybody laughed when he proudly put up a sign in his premises: 'Twenty-five years on the same spot.'

Clerk: Why do you always insist on taking your pay-packet to the bank as soon as we're paid?

Another Clerk: Because it's too small to go by itself.

The conscientious computer software company begged its customers: 'If any bugs in our software are bugging you, say so. You'll get it out of your system, and so will we.'

'What do you like most about being boss?' the new company chairman was asked.

After a thoughtful pause, the chairman replied: 'These days when I bore people they think it's their fault, not mine.'

When an employee went to the accounts department to get reimbursed for some travelling expenses, he was given a sheet of instructions. Looking the instructions over, he shook his head: 'Well, all right,' he said, 'but my boss is not going to like it.'

'What do you mean?' demanded the accountant.

The employee showed him one paragraph of the form: 'If an employee incurs reimbursable expenses, he must submit a completed expense voucher with the relevant receipts stapled to his department head.'

The busker in the underground was playing his heart out to very little effect until he put a neatly printed card on the floor near his hat: 'Hush money gratefully accepted.'

When the company chairman called in an industrial psychologist to give his employees the once over, he insisted on taking the tests himself.

The psychologists found the chairman's responses very enlightening, especially one:

Question: What is your usual reaction to criticism.

Answer: Extreme surprise.

Bank sign: 'Bring your business account here. Others may pay attention, but our interest is greater.'

A shopowner was complaining to a friend about how poorly his business was doing.

'I used to have that problem,' said the friend, 'but I came up with a very simple solution.'

'And what's that?' asked the intrigued shopkeeper.

'The secret is to work only half days.'

'Only half days? That's amazing.'

'And the best thing,' his friend continued, 'is that it doesn't matter which twelve hours you work.'

The company had recently cut its commission to salesmen, and some of them weren't at all happy about it.

On Monday, the sales manager greeted one of them by saying: 'I say, Carson, we seem to have issued your commission cheque a bit late last Friday. I hope you didn't have any trouble getting it cashed.'

'Oh, no,' said Carson, 'I swapped it for a newspaper on the way home.'

'What's this big item?' the boss demanded of his rep covering the northeast, as he looked over his latest expense account.

'Oh,' said the rep, 'that's just my restaurant bill.'

'I see,' said the boss doubtfully. 'Well, in future, don't buy any more restaurants.'

The wife ringing a week-end business conference with an urgent message for her husband, described him in vain: middle-aged, balding, getting fat, wearing a dark suit, striped tie and white shirt.

'I'm sorry,' said the receptionist, 'most of the men at the conference look like that. Can't you provide any more specific description?'

'Well,' said the embarrassed wife, 'he does have two

cute little moles on his right hip, but ...'

The receptionist interrupted her, exclaiming: 'Of course! I'll put you right through.'

'We'd like to give you the loan you request,' said the bank manager to the businessman, 'but what assurance can you give that it will be repaid on time?'

'Won't a gentleman's word of honour do?' asked the businessman.

'Of course,' said the bank manager. 'When will you be bringing him in?'

'I'm a bit worried, Jenkins,' said the boss, 'that your grandmother should need you to take her to the doctor every time there is an important cricket match.'

'I hadn't thought of that, sir,' said the habitual absentee. 'You don't suppose that she's faking it, do you?'

The proud father of a new-born daughter went into his bank to open an account for the new arrival, but he was stumped when he came to the part of the application which asked: 'Occupation.'

After thinking for a long moment, he wrote: 'Alarm clock.'

'I say,' said one stockbroker to another, 'does it seem to you that Carruthers is looking a bit unfit these days?'

'Yes,' said his colleague, 'and no wonder. The only exercise he gets is wrestling with his conscience, and he always throws the match.'

The applicant for a job with the bottled-water company came in for his interview and proudly handed over his qualifications to the personnel manager.

The personnel manager looked them over for a while and glanced up at the applicant. 'These swimming certificates are very impressive, Mr Oldfield, but we were rather hoping you could *sell* our product, not swim in it.'

Uncertain as to whether he could claim a certain business deduction from his taxes, the merchant telephoned his local tax office and launched into a long-winded description of the expense, the circumstances and why he felt that this was a justified deduction. Finally, he finished, and back came the answer: 'No.'

The businessman was about to hang up when he heard: 'This is a recorded announcement.'

The salesman knocked on a door and had barely started his spiel when the householder's three dogs ran in from the other room and set up such a racket that not a word could be heard. After several attempts, all of them drowned by the yapping, the salesman picked up his case and walked away without another word.

But to his surprise, the householder, after shutting the dogs in the house, followed the salesman to the pavement, and said: 'I'm a salesman myself, and I think you gave up too easily just then.'

'Think so?' said the door-to-door salesman. 'I'm selling burglar alarms.'

The lawyer's secretary discovered a leak in the restroom, so she called a plumber. After what seemed like seconds, the leak was stopped and the plumber handed in his bill, which the secretary passed on to her boss.

'I say,' said the lawyer, 'this bill of yours is rather steep for such a short time. Even *I* don't charge that much an hour.'

'I know,' said the plumber. 'I didn't, either, when I was a lawyer.'

Over a period of time, the employees of a small insurance office began to come to work consistently late. Then one day, there appeared on the front counter a beautifully wrapped gift. All day, the office workers gossiped about the mysterious parcel, but it wasn't until just before closing time that one of the employees worked up the courage to ask the boss what it was and who it was for.

'Oh,' he said, 'that's a leaving present for the very next person who comes in late.'

Old Hastings was guest of honour at his retirement dinner when the managing director – having had more than a little to drink – stood up to make the presentation. 'Hastings,' he said, 'as a token of our appreciation for your contribution to the firm over the last forty years, we had a very special gold watch made up for you. It needs a lot of winding up, it's always late, and every day at a quarter to five it stops working.'

Alf, one of two partners in a profitable house-painting business was putting on his overalls one day when Wilf, the other partner, came in and said: 'Alf, forget the Acme job today. I want the crew to go and do the Swift's Crisps factory all over again.'

'But, Wilf,' said his partner, 'we just finished that job yesterday, and they paid us. Why do it again?'

'Well,' said Wilf, 'you know how we've been mixing our paint with water so that it goes further?'

'Ssshhhh,' said Alf, looking around nervously. 'Don't say that out loud. Of course I know it, but nobody else does. What's the matter with you?'

'Well,' said Wilf, 'last night I woke up at 2 a.m. and there was an angel by the side of my bed.'

'An angel!' explained Alf. 'That's amazing. But what's that got to do with doing a big job all over again?'

'It's what the angel told me,' Wilf insisted. 'He looked at me with those big innocent blue eyes and said: "Repaint, you thinner!"'

Clearly in sight of all of the bank's tellers is a prominent sign: 'To err is human; to forgive is not bank policy.'

Invariably, the boss scheduled his staff meetings at 4:30 on a Friday afternoon. Finally one of his employees got up the nerve to ask him why.

'I'll tell you, Smith,' said the boss. 'I tried almost every other time of week before I settled on that particular time because I find that that's when nobody ever seems to want to argue with me.'

The Roman Emperor was advised that the way to make a lot of money was to build an amphitheatre and put on lavish shows for his subjects, so he did. But to his surprise, the new amphitheatre lost money from the very beginning.

Going to his manager, the Emperor demanded: 'See here, why aren't you making the money I was promised?'

'Well, you see, sire,' quavered the manager, 'it's this way: the lions are eating up all the prophets.'

'Now be honest, Reilly,' the boss demanded one evening when he was in his cups. 'Do my employees like me?'

'To be absolutely candid, boss,' said Reilly, who'd had a few himself, 'they don't.'

'But, why?'

'Well,' said Reilly, throwing caution to the wind, 'you're rude, aggressive, overbearing, dictatorial and arbitrary.'

The boss sat stunned into silence for a moment. Finally he said in a hurt voice: 'Well, sure, but only when people disagree with me.'

'You're famous for your Christian charity, Perkins,' said one gossiping employee to another, 'but I defy you to find anything good to say for young Jameson,' their boss's arrogant, opinionated, big-headed, over-educated son who'd just joined the firm after a long career as a professional student.

Perkins thought for a long time before he said: 'He may not be very smart, but he's got more degrees than a thermometer.'

New Secretary: 'Are the executives in this company easy to work for?'

Old Hand: 'Let me put it this way: around here, egos expand to fill the office space assigned to them.'

The boss wasn't known for his powers of diplomacy. At the retirement dinner for a long-time employee, he stood up and told the audience: 'We're really going to miss our old friend Pete Peterson. He'll be a hard man to replace at the pitiful salary we've been paying him all these years.'

The personnel director of a far-out advertising agency looked up from the applicant's CV and said: 'Your education is first-rate, your experience in the business is awesome, and your references are brilliant, but we were hoping for a Sagittarius with Gemini in the ascendency.'

Man to sympathetic bartender: 'I'm cursed with a terrible disposition, and unfortunately it happens to belong to my immediate boss.'

St Peter and the Devil set up rival companies, and the Devil accepted a contract to provide Heaven with the heat it needed. But then he demanded more money or no heat would be forthcoming.

'You fulfill our contract right now,' St Peter demanded, 'or I'll sue you.'

'I don't think so,' said the Devil confidently. 'I've got all the lawyers.'

The publisher's secretary came into his office: 'I'm sorry, sir,' she said, 'but one of your authors is on the phone.'

The publisher grabbed the telephone: 'Oh, hello, Peter, it's lovely to hear your voice. What can I do for you?'

'I'm calling about that manuscript I sent you some months ago,' said the author.

The publisher couldn't even remember it but he said: 'Of course. Of course. But remind me: is it an historical novel?'

'No,' the author replied drily, 'or at least it wasn't when I sent it to you.'

First Entrepreneur: 'I've got a terrific new project. I'm going to open a bar and grill in the middle of the Sahara Desert.'

Second Entrepreneur: 'That's a terrible idea. Nobody in his right mind crosses the Sahara. You'll be lucky to get a single customer.'

First Entrepreneur: 'Possibly, but if one does turn up, just think how thirsty he'll be!

The boss read the letter he'd just dictated and said: 'Miss Ferguson, I know I told you that this letter was confidential, but you didn't have to type it with your eyes shut.'

The office manager was showing visitors through the vast typing pool when one of the guests asked: 'How many secretaries work here?'

'Oh, about one in five, on average,' said the manager.

The travelling salesman checked into his usual hotel in the West Country but was behaving most strangely: he took the cheapest room in the house, ignored the cheeky badinage of the sexy blonde receptionist, ordered the special-offer menu instead of his usual steak and didn't order a single drink.

'What's got into you, Jack?' asked the jovial hotel manager when the salesman's dinner partner was away from the table. 'You don't seem yourself.'

'It's not what got into me, Phil,' said the salesman, 'it's what got into my car at headquarters – the sales manager.'

Dictating Executive: 'Have you got that, Miss Robinson?'

Secretary: (reading from notebook) 'Let's see: "Letter to old what's-his-name, look up the firm's name and address, usual salutation followed by standard opening paragraph, etc., etc., etc., throw in a few statistics, blah, blah, blah, a bit of flattery and finishing with the routine ending."'

Executive: 'That sounds about right. Type it up, will you?'

Sign on Cluttered Desk: 'A clean desk may show efficiency, neatness and organisation but very seldom provides a worthwhile surprise.'

The newly hired employee of the super-modern multinational was taken to his office and was surprised to find that it contained only two objects: the most high-tech computer he'd ever seen and a big, vicious guard dog.

'There you are,' said his guide. 'Your only job is to give the dog plenty of food and water and keep him in good condition. Any questions?'

'Well, yes,' said the new man, 'I do have one. What's the dog for?'

'The dog,' the guide explained, 'is here to keep you away from the controls of our computer!'

During the McCarthy era in the United States, a super-patriotic company demanded that its employees fill out a lengthy 'loyalty' form which included the following question:

'Do you support the overthrow of the United States government by subversion, violence or insurrection?'

A recent college graduate, used to multiple-choice examinations, responded: 'Violence.'

The new secretary got in the queue at the office paper shredder with some documents in her hand, but confessed that she didn't know how to operate the

machine. An old hand showed her which button to push, but as she was leaving the room, she heard the shredder begin to whirr, and the new secretary say: 'Now, I wonder how I set it to make six copies.'

When the secretary came in on Monday morning, she stared at her overflowing desk with amazement.

'What's the matter?' asked her boss.

'I swear,' said the secretary, 'that those papers breed over the weekend.'

The executive came upon an unexpected appointment in his Filofax.

'Who is *this*' he demanded of his secretary, 'you've got down for 2:45 to 2:55 next Wednesday afternoon after the lunch with the auditors and the merger meeting with Amalgamated Widgets? Who is Mrs Parkinson?'

'It's your wife, Mr Parkinson,' said his weary secretary. 'She said she had to see you, and that's the first time I could fit her in.'

Said the dissatisfied boss to his employee: 'You're fired. I've told Accounting to make out your final cheque.'

Half an hour later, the employee was about to leave with his few effects in a shopping bag, when the boss stopped him. 'Where do you think you're going?'

'Home. You fired me, didn't you?'

'Just like you,' said the boss. 'Any excuse to get the afternoon off, eh?'

'What I can't stand about Mr Figgis,' said the girl from the secretarial pool, 'is his big head.'

'What do you mean?'

'Well, I was looking through his files for a paper I needed, and I came across a file marked: "Mistakes." It was empty.'

Executive interviewing a student for a summer job: 'So, you're looking for some work experience, are you?'

Student: 'I suppose so, but what I really want is some earning experience.'

At the coffee machine, one employee said to another: 'I understand the company is looking for a treasurer.'

'I thought we hired one just last month,' said his colleague.

'That's the one they're looking for.'

The greengrocer got fed up with students parking their bicycles blocking his display so he put up a sign: 'Cycles left here will be recycled.'

The Texas oil man threw himself into the dentist's chair. 'Right,' he said, 'drill away'.

But after the dentist had examined the oil man's teeth, he said: 'I'm sorry. Your teeth are perfect. You don't need a thing.'

'That's okay,' said the millionaire. 'I feel lucky. Drill anyway.'

The super-salesman was being interviewed about his great success. 'I suppose,' he said, 'three of the principal rules of good salesmanship are: make lots of calls, know your product and never take no for an answer, but to be honest, I owe my success to knowing how to miss a three-foot putt by two inches.'

The successful executive not only got his personal assistant to write his speeches, but, knowing that they would be brilliant, didn't even bother to read them over before giving them.

Then, at the firm's big annual gathering he was on the platform delivering his speech when he got to the bottom of a page which concluded: 'And this leads me to three vital points ...' When he turned over, the executive found a totally blank page except for the words: 'I quit. You're on your own from here on.'

An Arab sheikh greeted his eldest son who had just returned from college in the United States. 'Well, my boy, what did you find most remarkable about the Americans: their democratic system, the easy equality among the classes, their spirit of initiative?'

'Well, father,' said the prince, unpacking six pairs

of snow shoes, 'those were all very interesting, but what I was most impressed by was their salesmanship.'

Customer in a second-hand bookshop: 'I haven't got much money, but I'm looking for a good book.'
Proprietor: 'Try one of these over here. They were owned by a little old lady who only read on Sunday.'

The company was involved in a serious lawsuit in Scotland, and a junior executive was sent to sit in the courtroom and observe the proceedings. As soon as the jury had made its decision, the junior executive jumped for the telephone and phoned the company chairman.

'It's Winterton,' he said excitedly down the phone. 'Justice has been done!'

'You get back in there, Winterton,' growled the chairman, 'and tell those lawyers to lodge an appeal immediately.'

Looking over the efficiency report on a new employee, the boss added at the bottom: 'It's obvious that Snodgrass is a real asset to the firm. He's efficient, punctual, loyal and imaginative. Perhaps even more important, he makes the other employees very nervous.'

Shop steward to foreman: 'We don't mind the pay cut, the faster assembly line or even the loss of our 15-minute washing-up time, but what's this new rule that you've got to be ill to take a day off sick?'

Definition of a statistician: Someone who, if he had his head in a coal fire and his feet in a block of ice would say: 'On average, I feel just fine.'

Sam was sitting sadly at the deathbed of his business partner, Bernie. With his last reserves of strength, Bernie raised his head from the pillow.

'Sam ... Sam ...'

'Rest, rest, Bernie,' Sam counselled. 'Save your energy.'

'No,' insisted the dying man. 'I can't. I must clear my conscience before I die. I've been a lousy partner, Sam. A lousy partner. It was me who sold the secret formula to Birmbaum; it was me who stole the £100,000 from the safe; it was me who reported to you to the tax inspectors ... It was me!'

'Don't bother yourself, Bernie,' said Sam. 'Don't worry. It was me who tampered with the brakes on your car.'

At the Ideal Home Show, the manufacturer of bathroom scales was proudly showing off its latest model.

'Now, this scale,' said the company chairman, 'has more high-tech features than any of the competition: calibration to the last hundredth of an ounce, human-voice simulator, capacity to register height as well as weight and a host of other unique capacities.'

'That's very impressive,' said the female executive of a national department store chain who could not really be called thin, 'and I'm very tempted to order thousands, but first I'd like to see it in action.'

'Help yourself,' said the chairman of the scale company.

But no sooner had the executive stepped on the scale, than it announced in a very human, very loud voice: 'One at a time, please. One at a time!'

The businessman was delighted when he heard that the tax office had developed a new, simplified tax form with only two questions on it. That is, until he got it:

1. How much did you make last year?
2. How much did you *really* make last year?

Now send us 35 per cent of the largest of these two figures.

A friend visiting a seriously ill corporate lawyer was surprised to find him leafing feverishly through a large Bible.

'What are you doing?' asked the visitor.

'Looking for loopholes,' said the lawyer, still searching.

The head of the company's training department sent out invitations to all of the other department chiefs to a seminar on the subject of 'Delegation.'

At the appointed hour, all of the seats in the lecture hall were filled, and the lecturer was about to begin when the chairman called aside the head trainer. 'Congratulations, Hobson,' he said. 'Your course is a terrific success.'

'Thank you, sir,' said the trainer, 'but it's not really begun yet.'

'You don't understand, man,' said the chairman. 'Look at your audience. Every single department head sent his deputy.'

Bright young thing to retired executive who'd come back for a company party: 'Didn't you use to be Mr Parkinson?'

The company's speaking computer was a sensation. So much so that executives kept it so busy answering trivial questions − just to hear it talk − that the work the computer had been bought to do didn't get done.

The head of the computer section got fed up with this and secretly programmed the talking computer with a special answer designed to discourage frivolous and unauthorised use.

The next day, the first person to come into the computer department was the company chairman. Before he could be stopped, the chairman asked the computer: 'What is our projected gross profit for this year?'

In response came the programmed answer: 'Stop wasting my time with stupid questions and go earn your salary.'

The lost traveller was crawling across the desert for the third straight day without water looking for an oasis when he saw a tiny speck coming towards him from the horizon. It got closer and closer until the thirsty traveller could see that it was a man with a suitcase.

'Water,' cried the traveller. 'For pity's sake – water.'

'I'm sorry,' said the man, opening his case, 'I don't have any, but can I sell you a tie?'

'No,' said the traveller.

'Are you sure?'

'Yes, I'm sure,' said the traveller and crawled on. Just over the next sand dune, he came upon a lovely oasis with a pool of beautiful, cool water, and standing at the gate of the oasis was a doorman.

'Water! Water!' croaked the parched traveller. 'I must have water.'

The doorman began to open the gate, but then he stopped and closed it. 'I'm sorry, sir,' he said, 'I can't let you in without a tie.'

'I need a good lawyer,' said the prospective client. 'The police have accused me of burgling a sporting goods shop.'

'I'll defend you,' said the lawyer, 'but it will cost you £150.'

'I haven't got it,' said the accused. 'Will you take £50 and a really nice set of golf clubs.'

The sales manager wondered why everybody laughed when he put up the sign: 'Salesmen without personal secretaries may take advantage of typists from the secretarial pool.'

The small-town businessman was up in London staying at a very posh hotel on Park Lane and wanted to make sure that he didn't make any gaffes, so he asked the head porter as he was about to check out: 'Tell me, how much is the acceptable tip from a guest staying here?'

'Fifty pounds, sir,' said the head porter.

This took the businessman aback, but he didn't want to seem cheap, so he handed the man £50, saying: 'You must be getting rich working here.'

'No, sir,' said the head porter, 'I've been working at

this hotel for fifteen years, and this is the first acceptable tip I've ever had.'

'Did you ever hear the like of it?' demanded a man of his mate. 'My son's gone into business on a shoestring and trebled his investment, but he's still not satisfied.'

'Why not?'

'He can't think of anything to do with three shoe-strings.'

The up-and-coming merchant banker splashed out on a Rolls Royce and offered a colleague a ride home from the office. As they were driving through the streets, the banker said proudly. 'What do you think of the Rolls? I suppose this is the first time you've ridden in one?'

'Not really,' said his passenger casually, 'but it's the first time I've ridden in the front seat.'

The customer was outraged to receive a letter from the accounts manager of his tailor, which said: 'Considering that we've done more for you than your mother did, we would be grateful if you would settle

your account immediately.'

'What do you mean you've done more for me than my mother?' he demanded.

'Well, sir,' said the manager, 'according to our files, we've been carrying you for fifteen months.'

Bank Customer: 'I've always wondered why you call them *Personal* Loans.'

Manager: 'That's because, madam, if you get behind in your payments, we tend to get a little personal.'

'It's that salesman from Acme Products on the phone,' the secretary told her boss.

'I'm a bit busy,' he said. 'Put him on hold with the Muzak tape for about ten minutes, and then if he's still there, I'll talk to him.'

The car salesman took a customer on a demonstration drive and was extolling the car's virtues. 'You could say,' he summed up, 'this automobile is the opportunity of a lifetime.'

'Yes,' said the would-be buyer, listening carefully, 'I can hear it knocking.'

'Say,' said the salesman trapping the firm's head buyer as he went out for lunch, 'I've been trying to see you for days to show you our new line.'

'Oh, make a date with my secretary,' said the buyer, trying to brush him off.

'I've had several dates with your secretary,' said the salesman, 'and they were great, but I still want to see you.'

Definition of success: When you jump out of bed at 7 a.m. every day shouting: 'Great, another day!' and then can afford to go back to bed.

Strap-hanging commuter, wearily: 'You know, I've been working all my life.'

Other commuter: 'Me too, but it seems longer.'

The plumber had been to look at a big job at the local convent and said that he'd send an estimate, but the nun couldn't wait and rang him. 'How much,' she asked, 'is it going to cost?'

'Just a second,' said the plumber, reaching for the estimate. Looking at the amount, he said with concern: 'Are you sitting down, sister.'

'No,' she said, just as concerned, 'kneeling.'

'My son thinks I'm made of money,' the businessman told his secretary. 'Tonight I'm going to give him a talking to that will really teach him the value of a pound.'

'How did you make out?' asked his secretary the next day.

'Not so good,' said his boss. 'Now he wants his allowance in Deutschmarks.'

At a conference, the junior executive couldn't quite conceal a huge yawn.

'You know,' said the chairman censoriously, 'it's very difficult to succeed in business on less than eight hours of sleep a night.'

'I know,' said the young executive, 'but you try telling that to my six-month-old son.'

'Hopkinson,' said the office manager to the boss's nephew, 'those two wire baskets on your desk are supposed to say: 'IN' and 'OUT', not 'EASY COME' and 'EASY GO'.

An economist is a person who stands at the edge of a bottomless chasm whispering: 'You might consider being careful of that loose guard rail.'

Then when you fall, he shouts loudly after you: 'You can't say I didn't warn you!'

The junior taxman was amazed when the businessman who had come into the tax office so enraged actually parted with the tax examiner with a smile and a handshake. 'I don't know how you do it,' he said admiringly to his senior.

'The art of tax assessment,' the senior taxman said, 'lies in plucking the goose of the maximum amount of feather with the least amount of hissing.'

The three chief officers of the bank were working late and somehow managed to lock themselves in the vault. 'What will we do?' asked the chief teller.

'Don't worry,' said the manager. 'It's two o'clock, and the vault will open automatically in just six hours. We can while away the time easily enough. For the first two hours, I'll sing songs. Then, for the next two hours, Bixby will tell jokes. And Carson, for the last two you can tell sad stories. I've heard that you're good at that.'

So for the first two hours the manager sang all the songs he knew, and then the deputy manager told jokes. Finally it was the turn of Carson, but he said nothing.

'Well, Carson?' said the manager.

'I've thought of a very sad story, sir,' said Carson. 'Tomorrow is Saturday.'

The two industrial giants were both after the Acme Paint Corporation, and they arranged a meeting with the chairman of Acme to argue the matter out. But the bargaining had no sooner begun than one tycoon shouted at the other: 'You're a liar!'

The other responded: 'And you're a cheat!'

'Now that you two have identified each other,' said the paint company boss, 'let's get on with our business.'

The businessman dictated a stiff letter to a customer who hadn't paid his bill for six months, but his secretary brought it back after typing it.

'I think it's a bit strong, sir,' she said, so he took the letter back and struck out a few of the most pungent bits.

The secretary retyped the letter, but still was a bit worried that he had been too severe. 'Oh, all right,' he said, 'I'll tone it down, but he'll hardly know what I'm writing about at this rate.'

Again the secretary brought the retyped letter to him. 'Now, I guess that's mild enough,' the boss said, 'but you've made a couple of spelling mistakes. There's only one "l" in swindler, and you needn't capitalise the word "horsewhip".'

The junior clerk came out of his boss's office shaking his head.

'What happened?' asked the secretary.

'I'm not sure,' said the clerk, 'but I think I've been fired.'

'What do you mean, you don't know?'

'The boss just looked at me and said: "Anderson, I don't know how we're going to do without you, but from next week we're going to do our best."'

The salesman came back from calling on a big customer looking less than happy.

'What happened?' asked his secretary. 'Didn't you get an order?'

'As a matter of fact,' said the salesman, 'I got three: "Get your hat! Get out! And don't come back!"'

The self-employed roofer filled in his National Insurance Card with Green Shield Stamps instead of payment stamps and sent it in.

Hauled before the magistrate, he was told: 'You are fined £20 or one electric kettle.'

The company chairman sent out an urgent memo to all of his executives: 'We must eliminate all unnecessary duplication of communication. I cannot repeat this too many times.'

The boss was interviewing a candidate for the job as his secretary and he asked her whether she had any special skills.

'Yes,' she said. 'Last year I won several short-story-writing contests and finished a novel.'

'That's very good,' said the boss, 'but I was thinking

about skills you could use during office hours.'

'Oh', said the prospect, 'that *was* during office hours.'

The company treasurer was asked for a reference by a former employee who hadn't exactly been a whizz kid. After thinking for a long time, he wrote: 'Mr Barnstaple worked for me a long time, and when you have known him as long as I have, you will probably share my opinion of him.'

The executive rang another department head angrily: 'When you sent me that fellow Cunningham, you told me he was a responsible worker.'

'He is,' said the department head, 'in the year he was in this department, our petty cash box got lost, the computer broke down, and I nearly had a nervous breakdown. And in each instance, Cunningham was responsible.'

The bank inspector was amazed to find the small-town bank open but apparently unmanned. There was nobody on either side of the counter. Prowling warily through the bank he at last looked in the vault and there were the manager, his assistant and the two tellers playing poker.

Backing quietly out into the main room of the bank, the inspector set off the alarm. To his surprise, nobody came out of the vault, but in a couple of minutes a waiter from the café across the street came in with beer and sandwiches.

A gift had been bought for the boss's departing secretary, and the receptionist was wondering where to hide it until the presentation at closing time.

'Put it in my filing cabinet,' said the boss. 'She was never able to find anything in there.'

The stockbroker arrived home from the office only to have his wife tell him that she had made an appointment for him at the blood bank.

'Fine,' he said, 'I could use a bit of new blood.'

'Golf, golf, golf,' complained the young bride at the breakfast table at the honeymoon hotel. 'All you've done since we got here is play golf. If I hear one more word about that game, I'm getting a divorce.'

'Darling,' the bridegroom assured her soothingly, 'golf is the furthest thing from my mind right now.'

But then he spoiled everything by adding: 'Could you please pass the putter?'

The secretary addicted to horoscopes described her boss to a friend in the company cafeteria: 'Just my luck,' she said. 'If he'd only been born three days later, he would have been patient, generous and thoughtful.'

The hotel chambermaid was breaking in a new employee and together they took breakfast to a travelling salesman's room. He was in the bathroom, and as she laid his breakfast tray, she called out: 'Do you have sugar in your coffee?'

Just as the salesman shouted: 'No, thanks,' the chambermaid noticed that the new girl had put two heaping spoons of sugar in the coffee.

'That's all right,' she told her. 'Just don't stir it.'

Salesman: 'We stand behind every vehicle we sell.'
Customer: 'Yes, but will you help push?'

The bank manager considered the rather shabby applicant for a £100 loan carefully. 'We might be willing to advance this money, but do you have any security? For instance, do you own a car?

'Yes,' said the applicant, 'an '89 Porsche.'

The bank manager's eyebrows rose at this, but he continued: 'Stocks or shares?'

'Of course,' said the applicant. 'I have quite a portfolio.'

'And do you own a house?'

'Yes, one with ten acres, a pool and tennis courts, actually.'

'You must be joking!' exclaimed the bank manager.

'Well, you started it,' said the applicant.

'I'm sorry,' said the bank teller refusing a customer's cheque, 'your account is overdrawn by £150.'

'That's impossible,' the customer said indignantly, 'I haven't got that much money.'

'Don't you feel intimidated having a university graduate for your secretary?' one executive asked another.

'No, it's wonderful,' replied his co-worker. 'When I'm dictating, she never asks me how to spell words, and I never have to admit that I don't have a clue.'

The sales manager was amazed to hear his secretary answer the telephone and say: 'I'm sorry, Sylvia, I can't talk to you right now. It's my lunch hour, but I'll ring you as soon as it's over.'

The successful businessman was giving his son a lecture: 'In business, ethics are very important. For instance, a customer comes in and pays a £20 account in cash. Just after he leaves, you notice that he's given you two £20 notes stuck together. Immediately you are faced with a basic ethical question: Should I tell my partner?'

'I thought you said you could type 80 words a minute,' the executive complained to his secretary, who seemed to be taking forever on the letter he'd dictated.

'Well, yes, I can,' said the secretary defensively, 'some minutes, but not all of them.'

The lightbulb above the executive's desk burnt out, and he sent for a maintenance man to change it. When the maintenance man began to climb up on his expensive desk in filthy boots, the executive asked him: 'Wouldn't you like a piece of paper to stand on?'

'That's all right, Guv,' said the worker, 'I can reach it from here.'

At the tax office an inspector answered the telephone, listened for a moment and then said: 'If you can't stop crying for just a moment, sir, I won't even know who you are.'

The lobster had been forced to borrow from a loan shark and was being pressed hard to pay up. The worried crustacean was about at the end of his tether when he spotted a squid racked with a terrible cough.

'You don't look too clever, mate,' said the lobster.

'I feel terrible,' said the squid. 'I think I have flu.'

'Come with me,' said the lobster, grabbing the squid's tentacle in a claw.

The squid felt so bad that he didn't even notice that he was being towed right up to the shark, until the lobster flung him into the predator's gaping jaws, shouting: 'All right, here's the sick squid I owe you, now lay off!'

The restaurateur looked down from his office and saw the headwaiter listening attentively to a couple of customers. In a minute, the headwaiter was knocking on his door. 'I've got some complaining customers, he said.

'What's their problem?' the restaurateur asked.

'They say the food is terrible,' said the headwaiter, 'and what's more, the portions are too small.'

The new assistant was left in charge of the green-grocer's shop for the first time when a really tough looking man came in and demanded half a cabbage.

'I'm sorry,' said the assistant nervously, 'I'm not allowed to cut the cabbages. The owner says ...'

'I don't care what the owner says,' growled the thug.

'You cut me half a cabbage right now or I'll take this place apart.'

'Just a second, sir,' said the intimidated boy, and he walked to the back of the shop where his employer was washing vegetables.

'Hey, boss,' the boy said, 'there's a real moron out there who wants me to sell him half a cabbage ...' But then he noticed that the menacing customer had followed right behind him. Quickly he added: '... and this gentleman would like the other half.'

The one thing that disturbed the boss was coming into the office and finding all of the employees he paid to work just sitting around gossiping and not working, so he called together his entire staff.

'Now, see here,' he told them, 'I'm a fair sort of chap, and I know there must be a better way to organise things so that when I arrive in the morning I don't find you just wasting time. So I'm putting up a suggestion box, and I hope that I'll find the answer in it.'

At the end of the day when everybody had gone home, he opened up the suggestion box and to his surprise found only a single slip of paper in it with the following typed on it: 'Stop wearing rubber-soled shoes.'

'I thought you'd got a job,' said one regular in the dole queue to another.

'So did I,' said his companion. 'They made me shave off my moustache and beard and then they didn't like the look of my face.'

The bright young man had done so well at the iron-monger's shop that his boss said: 'I think you've got a great deal of promise. How would you like to manage my store in Cardiff?'

'Cardiff?' exclaimed the young man, taken by surprise. 'Nobody lives in Cardiff but dummies and rugby players.'

'I'll have you know, young man,' said the boss, 'that my wife comes from Cardiff.'

The bright young man recovered quickly, asking: 'And what position does she play?'

'How's your daughter getting along with her summer job with your firm?' the company president's friend asked him.

'I'll tell you,' the president said, 'I've had all kinds of labour problems in my business career, but this is the first time I've had an employee appeal against my decisions to her mother.'

'You're late,' said the golfer to his partner.

'Sorry,' said the tardy one, 'but it was a toss up whether I'd come at all or go to the office, and I had to toss up fifteen times.'